Christmas Carols For Clarinet With Piano Accompaniment Sheet Music Book 3

Michael Shaw

Copyright © 2015 Michael Shaw. All rights reserved. Including the right to reproduce this book or portions thereof, in any form. No part of this text may be reproduced in any form without the express written permission of the author.

Music Arrangements. All Christmas Carol arrangements in this book by **Michael Shaw Copyright © 2015**

ISBN: 1517100348
ISBN-13: 978-1517100346

www.mikesmusicroom.co.uk

Contents

Introduction	
O Little Town Of Bethlehem: Clarinet	1
O Little Town Of Bethlehem: Clarinet & Piano	2
O Come O Come Emmanuel: Clarinet	4
O Come O Come Emmanuel: Clarinet & Piano	6
The Gloucestershire Wassail: Clarinet	9
The Gloucestershire Wassail: Clarinet & Piano	10
It Came Upon The Midnight Clear: Clarinet	13
It Came Upon The Midnight Clear: Clarinet & Piano	14
Go Tell It On The Mountain: Clarinet	17
Go Tell It On The Mountain: Clarinet & Piano	18
Gather Around The Christmas Tree: Clarinet	21
Gather Around The Christmas Tree: Clarinet & Piano	22
O Holy Night: Clarinet	24
O Holy Night: Clarinet & Piano	26
Good Christian Men Rejoice: Clarinet	30
Good Christian Men Rejoice: Clarinet & Piano	32
Angels From The Realms Of Glory: Clarinet	35
Angels From The Realms Of Glory: Clarinet & Piano	36
Unto Us A Boy Is Born: Clarinet	38
Unto Us A Boy Is Born: Clarinet & Piano	39
About The Author	42

Introduction

The sheet music in this book has been arranged for Clarinet. There are two versions of every piece in this book. The first version is a Clarinet only arrangement, the second version is a Clarinet and piano accompaniment arrangement. Both versions are for beginners and easy to play. The piano parts in this book can be played on a piano, keyboard or organ.

Versions Of This Book For Other Instruments

As well as playing duets with piano in this book you can also play together in a duet or ensemble with other instruments with a sheet music book for that instrument.

To get a book for your instrument choose from the Christmas Carols With Piano Accompaniment Book 3 series. Instruments in this series include, Trombone, Oboe, Flute, Alto Saxophone, Tenor Saxophone, French Horn and Trumpet. Please check out my author page on Amazon to view these books.

Author Page US
amazon.com/Michael-Shaw/e/B00FNVFJGQ/

Author Page UK
amazon.co.uk/Michael-Shaw/e/B00FNVFJGQ/

O Little Town Of Bethlehem

Arr. Michael Shaw — Clarinet — Traditional

O Little Town Of Bethlehem

Arr. Michael Shaw
Clarinet & Piano
Traditional

O Come O Come Emmanuel

Arr. Michael Shaw

Clarinet

15th Century French

O Come O Come Emmanuel

Arr. Michael Shaw   Clarinet & Piano   15th Century French

The Gloucestershire Wassail

Arr. Michael Shaw
Clarinet
Traditional

The Gloucestershire Wassail

Arr. Michael Shaw
Clarinet & Piano
Traditional

It Came Upon The Midnight Clear

Arr. Michael Shaw
Clarinet
Traditional

It Came Upon The Midnight Clear

Arr. Michael Shaw
Clarinet & Piano
Traditional

Go Tell It On The Mountain

Arr. Michael Shaw · Clarinet · Traditional

Go Tell It On The Mountain

Arr. Michael Shaw — Clarinet & Piano — Traditional

19

Gather Around The Christmas Tree

Arr. Michael Shaw — Clarinet — Traditional

Gather Around The Christmas Tree

Arr. Michael Shaw

Clarinet & Piano

Traditional

O Holy Night

Arr. Michael Shaw

Clarinet

Adolphe Adam

O Holy Night

Arr. Michael Shaw

Clarinet & Piano

Adolphe Adam

Good Christian Men Rejoice

Arr. Michael Shaw
Clarinet
Traditional

Good Christian Men Rejoice

Arr. Michael Shaw Clarinet & Piano Traditional

34

Angels From The Realms Of Glory

Arr. Michael Shaw Clarinet Henry Smart

Angels From The Realms Of Glory

Arr. Michael Shaw

Clarinet & Piano

Henry Smart

Unto Us A Boy Is Born

Arr. Michael Shaw — Clarinet — Traditional

Unto Us A Boy Is Born

Arr. Michael Shaw
Clarinet & Piano
Traditional

About the Author

Mike works as a professional musician and keyboard music teacher. Mike has been teaching piano, electronic keyboard and electric organ for over thirty years and as a keyboard player worked in many night clubs and entertainment venues.

Mike has also branched out in to composing music and has written and recorded many new royalty free tracks which are used worldwide in TV, film and internet media applications. Mike is also proud of the fact that many of his students have gone on to be musicians, composers and teachers in their own right.

You can connect with Mike at:

Facebook
facebook.com/keyboardsheetmusic

Soundcloud
soundcloud.com/audiomichaeld

YouTube
youtube.com/user/pianolessonsguru

I hope this book has helped you with your music, if you have received value from it in any way, then I'd like to ask you for a favour: would you be kind enough to leave a review for this book on Amazon? It'd be greatly appreciated!

Thank You
Michael Shaw

Made in the USA
Las Vegas, NV
04 November 2023